Beginner's Guide to Building Ships in Bottles

William Sheridan

PublishAmerica
Baltimore

First printing

ISBN: 1-4241-7597-6 (softcover)
ISBN: 978-1-4489-0256-9 (hardcover)
PUBLISHED BY PUBLISHAMERICA, LLLP
www.publishamerica.com
Baltimore

Printed in the United States of America

Dedicated to: Nan, Billy and Meg

Preface

The centuries old craft of building a ship in a bottle is well known by most people, but very few have actually built one or even tried it. The art form is not meant for only sailors or expert modelers, this is a hobby that can be enjoyed by all types of people. The best way to start a new endeavor is by tackling something simple to ensure success.

The models presented here are simple enough for the beginner while still attractive enough for professional display. The goal is to get the young modeler or first time modeler to try it. All that is required are some basic hand tools, a few scraps of wood, paper, clay and a suitable bottle. Throw in some patience and a bit of creativity and you'll have a model worthy of displaying in a home or office.

I believe many will find this art form to be an interesting and enjoyable way to pass the time.

Table of Contents

List of Figures

Introduction

There are many myths and mysteries surrounding ship-in-the-bottle models. The first mystery, of course, is how to build the ship inside the bottle and that will be explained in great detail later in this book. A second myth is that the hobby is only meant for retired sea captains or those with highly specialized modeling skills, leaving the art to only a few select individuals. This is not true and can be explained by an analogy to sports or music. Everyone has a favorite professional athlete, entertainer or musician that is highly skilled at what they do. Even though there are only a small number of people who are tops in their field, it doesn't discourage others to try it themselves. For every professional golfer there are hundreds of weekend golfers who enjoy the sport even though their game isn't 100% perfect. So too it is with building a ship in a bottle. The model does not need to be a complex arrangement of sails and rigging, sometimes a simple vessel with one or two sails and a few lines can make an elegant showpiece in one's home or office. Another myth is that the boat must be a historic vessel or a ship with only square rigged sails. The second model described in this text is patterned after a modern sloop rig and the modeler is encouraged to design their boat after one they can find docked at the shore or perhaps parked on a trailer in their own backyard. Art does not have to be complex and can be enjoyed by even those with modest abilities. After all, even the experts needed to start somewhere and it's best to start simple.

This book is intended for the first time modeler, industrial arts student or the experienced ship modeler who hasn't built a ship in a bottle before. In the case of the student woodworker, these projects may be more fun than building the traditional birdhouse or napkin holder and really don't require much more in the way of woodworking skills. The reader is taken through the details of building two projects based on simple sailing rigs.

Step by step instructions are provided, starting with tools and materials and ending with final paint and installation. After finishing both projects, the modeler will understand all the basics behind building a ship in a bottle and will have the ability to create and devise their own simple models or tackle more advanced designs. There are many fine books written on the subject by talented craftsman, but the beginner may find it helpful to start with this book first before taking on more advanced and complex models.

The models contain very few parts and can be built in less than 20 hours of work. These models are scratch built from raw materials with plenty of room for creative alternatives and unique features. Detail drawings with dimensions are provided to help the first time modeler fashion the components to the correct scale. Building a model of your own design is much more satisfying than building a model from a kit.

Chapter 1
Project 1—Lateen Rig

The lateen rig is one of the oldest known sailing rigs in the world. Middle Eastern and Mediterranean sailors used it for centuries and it is still being sailed today on many small recreational boats. The basic lateen rig consists of a single mast and one triangular sail. Figure 1.1 shows a traditional Mediterranean fishing boat whose design essentially remained the same from the 3rd century to the19th century. As seen in the figure, the boat is based on extremely simple hull lines yet it is pleasant to look at. Project 1 will reproduce much of the detail from this boat, in miniature of course, capturing the graceful hull lines and rigging. The modeler will create the hull, seats, rudder, mast, sails, and even some passengers, all inside a small whiskey bottle.

To learn more about the history of this sailing vessel, please see the "Further Reading" section of this book. Before starting the project it's best to become familiar with the parts of the boat as described below.

Figure 1.2 may be helpful for those readers who are not familiar with basic sailboat terminology. The rudder is used to steer or change direction of the boat. It is attached to the stern (back) of the hull and is controlled by the tiller which is a wooden handle held by the helmsman or person who steers the boat. The mast is tipped forward and mounted in the middle of the hull as shown in the original model from Figure 1.1. The sail is attached to a wooden pole or spar and it is raised to the top of the mast by a rope called a halyard. The spar on a lateen rig is sometimes referred to as the yardarm. The spar can be adjusted at different angles to the mast by use of a separate halyard and is adjusted depending on the wind direction. The tack secures the front of the sail to the bow (front) of the hull. The main control for the sail is a rope called the mainsheet. With no tension on the mainsheet the sail will flap in the breeze like a flag. As tension is increased on the mainsheet, the sail will flatten to become an airfoil shape that is efficient enough to propel the boat through the water. When the sail is flapping in the breeze, it is said to be "luffing" and the boat will not make any forward progress. The mainsheet requires frequent adjustment by the helmsman or crew to ensure there is no "luff" in the sail. All of the parts in this figure will be constructed for the ship-in-the-bottle model.

Figure 1.1—Model of Mediterranean Fishing Boat
with Lateen Sailing Rig. (*Photo taken by the author*)

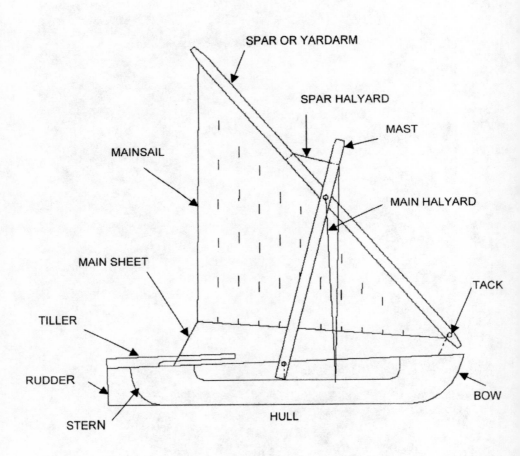

Figure 1.2—General Arrangement of Lateen Rig Fishing Boat

Chapter 2
Tools

Figure 2.1 shows a grouping of standard tools that the modeler will need to complete the project. These tools can be purchased at a hobby or hardware store for a modest cost. Since this book is intended for beginners, less costly hand tools can be used to complete all the work.

The essential tools consist of a coping saw, hand carving blades (X-acto brand), a ruler, pencil, tweezers, paint brushes, sand paper and a modeler's drill set, ranging from .25mm to 1.5mm in diameter. The more experienced modeler may have electric versions of these tools that are more expensive and higher quality, but they are not required to complete any of the projects in this book. Since tools can be used over and over again for many tasks, it is up to the modeler to decide how much of an investment should be made in standard tools.

There are two special tools needed for ship-in-the-bottle models. The modeler can create these tools from inexpensive household items. As shown in the lower part of Figure 2.1, the tools include; a wooden dowel of 6 to 8mm in diameter with an attached 12mm X 12mm X 25mm long rounded block. Note that the rounded block must be small enough to fit through the neck of the bottle. The second tool is a metal hook made of 3 mm diameter wire. The purpose of these tools will be explained in detail later in the book, but essentially they are used to insert and press clay within the bottle to form the ocean for the model. The metal hook will also be used to manipulate the ship inside the bottle and adjust the rigging prior to final installation.

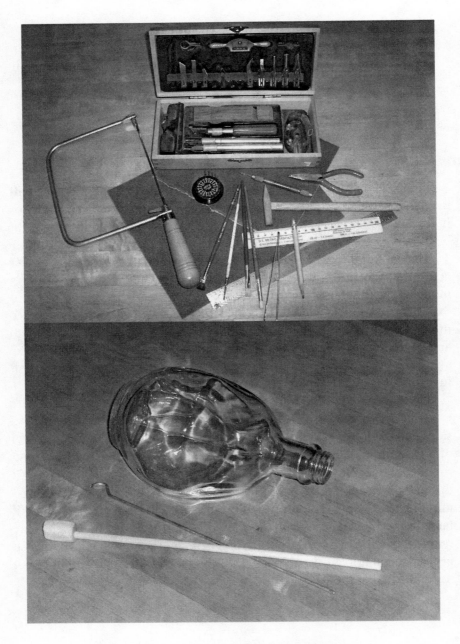

Figure 2.1—Tools for Building All Projects

Chapter 3
Materials

The same materials are used for both projects. Final dimensions are given in the chapters where the material is cut and shaped. Most of these items can be taken from small scraps of wood or other household items. There is no need to spend a lot of money obtaining materials.

- Wooden Block for the Hull—20mm X 20mm X 75mm
- Wooden Dowel for the Mast and Spar—2 mm in Diameter
- Wood Strips for the Seats, Rudder & Tiller—1.5mm X 6mm X 25mm
- Thin Cardboard Strips—½ mm thick
- Adhesive for Wooden Models
- High Quality Paper for the Sails—25% Cotton Rag Bond
- Black & White Thread
- Paints—White, Black, Red, Gray, Blue and Green
- Wood Stain—Natural Color of Your Choice
- Plastic N-Scale (Model Train)—Human Figures in the Sitting Position
- Non-Hardening Clay for Making the Ocean—Plasticine is suggested
- Round Metal Wire—1 mm in Diameter
- Clear Bottle—750 ml "Pinch" Scotch Whisky Bottle is Suggested
- Cork

Please note that all the dimensions are given in millimeters. For those who are more familiar with the English System of units, the following table will be helpful. Please note that the models will not be made to an exact scale, so rounding things off to a more convenient size is not an issue.

One Inch equals exactly 25.4mm.

Here is a list of **approximations** for working in English Units

½ mm ~ .020 inches
1 mm ~ .040 inches
2 mm ~ .080 inches
3 mm ~ 1/8 inch
6 mm ~ ¼ inches
12 mm ~ ½ inches
25 mm ~ 1 inch
50 mm ~ 2 inches

Chapter 4
Making the Hull

The wooden block for the hull can be made of soft wood that is easy to carve but strong enough to withstand some handling. The preferred woods to use are pine and aspen. Balsa wood is easy to work with, but it is extremely soft and may get damaged as you handle it during the latter part of the modeling process. Oak, maple, cherry and other hardwoods are very durable, but they can be difficult to cut and shape to the desired form.

Start by tracing the pattern on the wooden block and then cutting it to the shape shown in Figure 4.1. Using a coping saw cut the curved shape as shown in the top left view first. The interior of the hull can be hollowed out using a carving knife or small chisel. Don't worry about getting it perfect. Figure 4.2 shows what your hull might look like after roughing it out with the saw. Although power tools are not needed, it may be convenient to use a router to cut out the interior of the hull, as shown in the upper right corner of Figure 4.2. Trimming each end of the hull to the correct angle first forms the bow and stern. Then carve the edge of the hull to form a bevel shape. By using sand paper and files, the hull should be smoothed to the final shape as shown in the lower right corner of Figure 4.2.

After the hull is sanded to the desired shape, add the seats, rudder and pilot holes. Start by adding the rub rails to the side of the hull using a thin strip of cardboard. The cardboard or heavy paper should be ½ mm thick and 2 mm wide. It can be glued to the hull using a variety of adhesives obtained from a local hobby store. White glue works well with thin strips of material, but it takes a long time for the glue to set and hold. There are many fast setting liquid or gel adhesives that are designed to hold wood and paper and these are the preferred types of glues.

The holes for the rigging should be drilled as shown in Figure 4.3. All holes are 1mm in diameter and can be made with a small hand drill. Be careful to angle the holes so that they break through the bottom of the hull. These holes will be used to draw the lines of the rigging and will latter be hidden under the hull once it is installed in the bottle. The steering mechanism for the boat (rudder and tiller) is fashioned from small strips of wood (1.5mm thick) to the approximated shape shown in the figure. Don't worry about exact dimensions; just fashion the pieces to the best of your ability to match the drawing. Fit the rudder (5mm long) as best you can to the stern or rear of the boat using fast setting adhesive. The tiller (25mm long) is attached to the top of the rudder and sits flat across the back of the boat. After the rudder and tiller are complete, make the seats from thin strips of wood as shown in the figure and glue them securely with fast setting adhesive.

Once complete, the hull can be painted. The outside of the hull is white. The rub rails are red. The inside of the hull can be painted dark gray with white seats. The tiller can be stained to a natural wood color.

Refer to Figure 1.2 at the beginning of this book for a description of the parts of the boat mentioned in the instructions

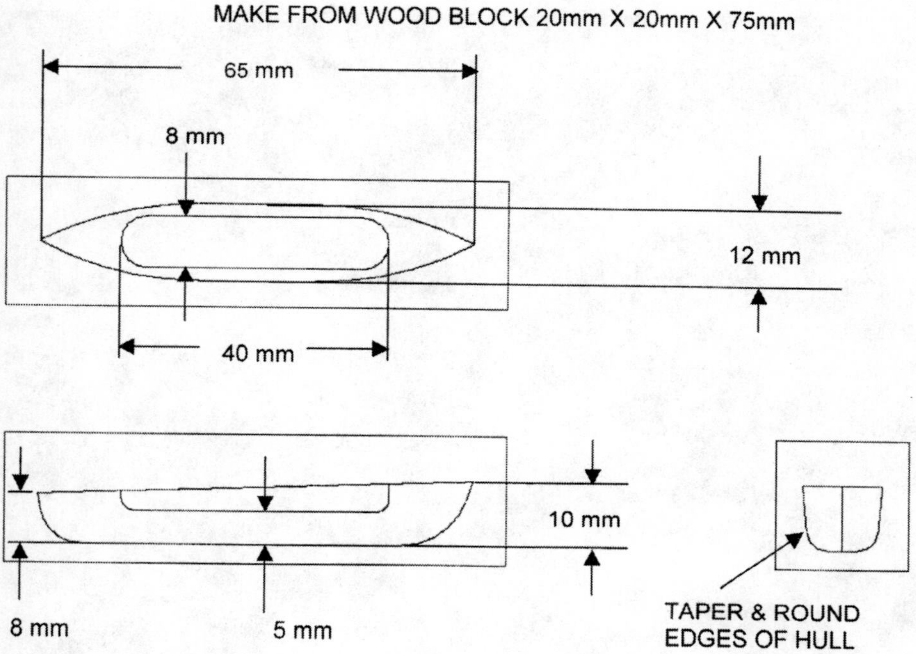

MAKE FROM WOOD BLOCK 20mm X 20mm X 75mm

Figure 4.1—Hull Dimensions and Plan View

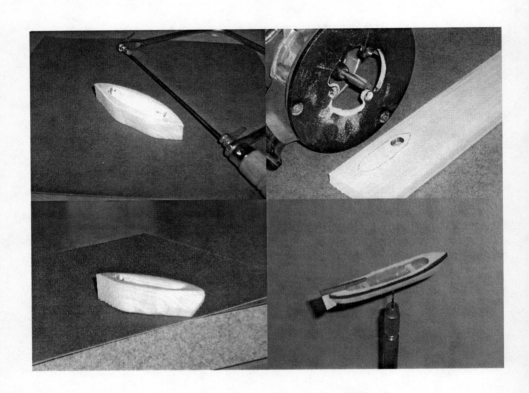

Figure 4.2—Steps in Creating the Hull

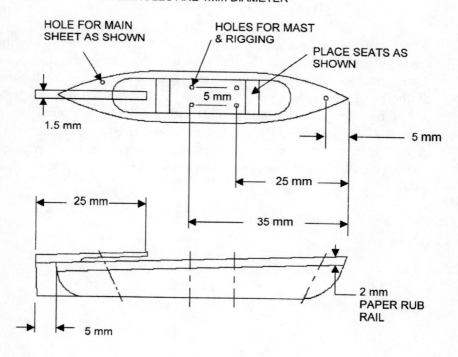

Figure 4.3—Details for Seats, Holes, Rudder and Tiller

Chapter 5
Making the Mast and Spar

The mast and spar are relatively easy pieces to make. Start with 2mm diameter round wood and cut the mast to 50mm long and the spar to 80mm in length. Taper and round off the ends of both pieces and then drill the holes as shown in Figure 5.1. Note that each piece has two holes drilled into the paper (perpendicular) and one hole in the plane of the paper (at right angles to the two other holes). If you are unsure of the pattern, refer to Figure 6.1 to see how the piece will fit together before drilling the holes. Sand each piece and stain them with a natural wood color.

MAST – 2mm DIAMETER BY 50mm LONG – ALL HOLES 1mm DIAMETER

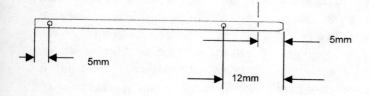

SPAR – 2mm DIAMETER BY 80mm LONG – ALL HOLES 1mm

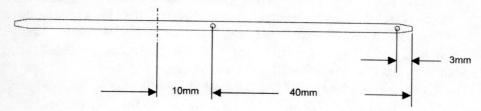

Figure 5.1—Mast and Spar Dimensions

Chapter 6
Attaching the Sails, Spar and Rigging

Figure 6.1 shows the secret behind making ships in a bottle! The mast is hinged so that it can fold down to allow it to be installed through the neck of the bottle and then raised once inside. Before going through the construction details, study Figures 6.2 to see how the mechanism works.

Using the 1mm diameter metal wire create the hinge as shown and fit it to the hull in the aft set of parallel holes spaced 5mm apart. The mast should swivel easily on the hinge so that it doesn't take a great amount of force to move it. A slight amount of friction is acceptable, but not desired, since the mast will be supported by rigging just as it would be in an actual sailing vessel. Make sure the mast swings directly aft and not to the side of the hull. This mechanism must fit through the neck of the bottle. Now may be a good time to trial fit the assembly partially in the neck of the bottle to make sure things will go together later.

Using 500mm lengths of black thread attach the spar to the mast as shown in Figure 6.1. The thread is securely tied to the spar and can be reinforced with a drop of glue to keep the knots tied. Slip the thread through the holes in the mast to form the two halyards. Halyards are ropes which are used to hoist sails and rigging. Do not put any glue on the holes in the mast! These holes must run free and clear to allow the halyards to raise and lower the sail mechanism. Likewise do not put any glue on the holes in the hull. After the halyards are complete, thread the hole for the tack (forward part of the sail). As a check, try to raise and lower the mechanism. If done properly the mast can be raised by gently pulling on the halyards from the bottom of the hull. In other words, you should be able to go from left to right in Figure 6.2 by simply pulling on the threads very gently forcing the mast to swivel upright on the hinge.

The sails are made from two pieces of good quality cotton rag paper. Do not use thin inexpensive paper; the paper must withstand the moisture from glue and also the test of time. The paper is cut into two 50mm X 50mm X 75mm triangles with a 500mm thread (main sheet) fitted between them as shown in Figure 6.2. The thread must be securely fastened between the sheets of paper since it will be under tension once the ship is installed in the bottle. The 75mm edge should have a V-shaped lip so that it can be attached to the spar as shown in the figure. Before gluing the sails, they can be weathered with a few drops of wood stain or coffee to give them a used appearance. Using a pencil or pen, seams can be traced on the sails so that they mimic the appearance of Figure 1.1. There is no right or wrong way to color the sails. They can be left pure white or colored to a dark brown or shade of gray. This is left up to the desires of the modeler. After the sails are colored and glued, the main sheet is threaded through the hull.

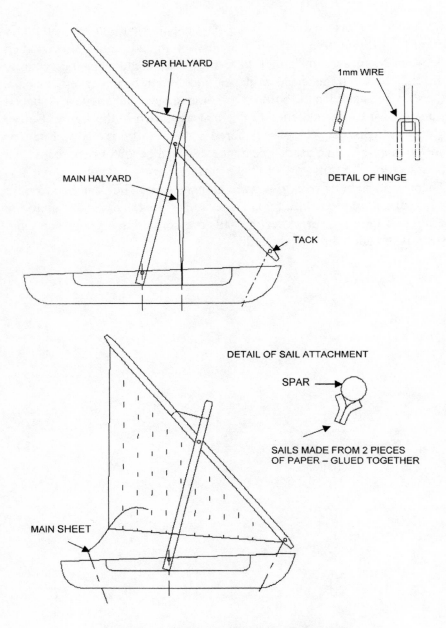

SPAR HALYARD

1mm WIRE

MAIN HALYARD

DETAIL OF HINGE

TACK

DETAIL OF SAIL ATTACHMENT

SPAR

SAILS MADE FROM 2 PIECES
OF PAPER – GLUED TOGETHER

MAIN SHEET

Figure 6.1—Mast, Sail and Spar Assembly

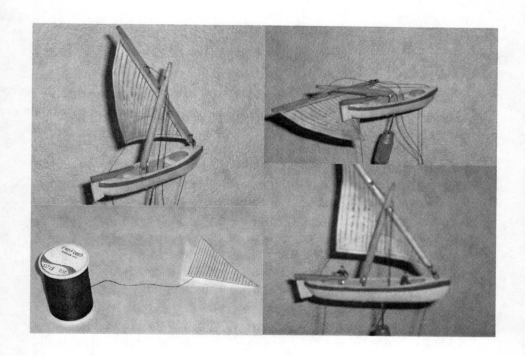

Figure 6.2—Fully Rigged Vessel Prior to Inserting in Bottle

Chapter 7
Fine Details

One of the easiest ways to include realistic detail to the model is by adding sailors to the boat. There are many types of model train accessories available including scaled human figures. The lower right corner of Figure 6.2 shows two N-Scale passengers sitting in the fore and aft seats of the fishing boat. Check with your local hobby store and try to find N-scale plastic human figures, which are in the sitting position. Simply remove them from the package and glue them to the desired position in the boat. For project 1, two figures were added as shown, but don't let that inhibit your creativity. Add as many figures to the boat as you wish. Likewise, you may add a coil of thread to simulate rope, or a piece of stocking to simulate a fishing net, needles to simulate harpoons and nearly anything else that might enhance the realistic look of the vessel.

See the further reading section of this book for getting other ideas to enhance your model. Ship Model Building by Gene Johnson is an excellent source for ideas and techniques for adding detail to your model.

Chapter 8
Preparing the Bottle

The choice of bottle is up to the modeler. For this project a 750 ml "Pinch" Scotch Whiskey bottle was used, but any clear bottle is acceptable. For the first time modeler it is suggested that the bottle have a short neck, so that it is easy to reach inside the bottle. It is also suggested to use flat-sided bottles so that the bottom and top are clearly defined. Round bottles roll around too much and are slightly harder to work with. After selecting the bottle, clean it thoroughly with warm soap and water. Remove all traces of glue by using isopropyl alcohol. The inside of the bottle can be cleaned with white vinegar to ensure a spot free appearance.

Select blue or aquamarine clay that is non-hardening so that it won't dry out or crumble over time. Plasticine is suggested. Roll it by hand as shown in Figure 8.1, so that the rolls will fit easily through the neck of the bottle. Press the clay into the bottom of the bottle using the special wooden dowel tool mentioned at the beginning of the book. Don't worry if the clay is not perfectly flat. The natural unevenness of the clay will simulate waves in the ocean. You may find it convenient to use a hair dryer to warm the bottom of the bottle during this process. Warm clay is easier to shape and form than cool clay.

After the bottom of the bottle is covered, use the wire hook tool to create a series of indentations across the entire clay surface. This will give the illusion of waves. See Figure 8.1 for the desired surface texture. Create a depression in the middle of the clay ocean slightly smaller than the length and width of the hull. The boat will be pressed into the clay and the initial depression is needed to ease the force needed to secure the hull.

Dab some white paint randomly around the clay ocean as shown in Figure 8.1, using a long handle paintbrush. You may attach the end of the paintbrush to the end of your wire tool. The wire tool can act as a variety of tools by attached items such as an X-acto blade shown in Figure 9.1. Finally add a little extra white paint at the front and rear of the depression to simulate the bow wave and wake of the vessel. If you find that you've spread too much white paint on the surface, let it dry and then go over it again with the wire hook tool. The tool will drive the paint beneath the surface of the clay and create a fresh surface.

During this entire process it is important to keep the sides of the bottle clean from clay and paint smudges. So it is important to be careful when inserting anything inside the bottle. Since no one is perfect, the wire hook tool is a good device to scrap excess paint from the sides of the bottle. You can also attach a small piece of cotton to the end of the tool and dab it in white vinegar to remove small smudges from inside the bottle.

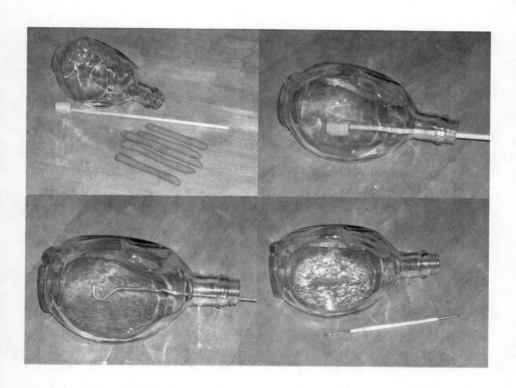

Figure 8.1—Preparing Clay (Plasticine) for Insertion

Chapter 9
Project 1—Final Installation

Final installation can begin once the white paint has dried on the clay. Start by folding the mast and rigging so that it will easily fit through the neck of the bottle as shown in Figure 9.1. Make sure the four black threads are pulled away from the hull and will dangle outside the neck of the bottle.

Since you will eventually need to press the hull into the clay, it is highly recommended to warm the bottle and clay ocean with a hair dryer so that the clay will be soft enough to form and excess force will not be needed to manipulate the ship inside the bottle.

Slide the ship through the neck of the bottle and let it fall into the middle of the clay ocean. Pull the four threads out the neck of the bottle and separate them so that you can tell which are the halyards, tack and mainsheet. Using the wire hook manipulate the hull into the depression and press down firmly so that the hull will stick into the clay. Hold the hull down into the clay with the wire hook and pull the four threads a little bit at a time until all the slack and tension is removed. Use the wire tool to prop up the mast and pull the main halyard until it is tight. Next pull the tack until the front of the sail and spar are positioned closely against the bow of the hull. Pull the spar halyard so that the sail is positioned as shown in Figure 9.1. Finally pull the main sheet so that all slack and tension is removed. Patience and gentleness are key elements in this final process. If the ship does not behave properly carefully pull it out of the bottle using all four lines and try it again. If the initial depression was too big or too small, reform it with the wire tool and try the process again.

When pulling each line, you'll note that the clay acts as a natural friction lock. Since the lines are running under the hull, the clay works like glue to hold them in place. After the sail is adjusted, reach carefully into the bottle with a small paintbrush and add a dab of white glue to each line where it joins the spar and runs through the hull to ensure that it won't loosen up later on. Pull all four lines tightly as shown in Figure 9.1 and tape them to the outside neck of the bottle. Let the glue dry and let the clay cool down to room temperature to ensure the hull and rigging is stable.

When everything is dry reach into the bottle with an X-acto knife and cut the four threads at the water line of the hull. If excess thread is protruding above the clay, reach in with the wire tool and press the thread gently into the clay so that it is hidden from view. Add a few dabs of white paint to cover up any traces of the lines or unsightly depressions from the wire hook.

Let the whole model dry for 24 to 48 hours to ensure that no moisture builds up within the bottle. Finish the model with a cork as shown in Figure 9.1.

Congratulations! You've built your first ship-in-a-bottle!

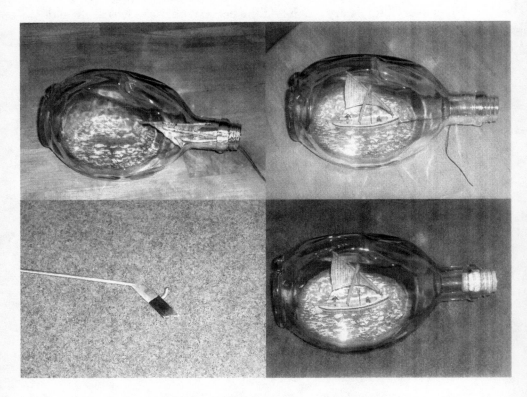

Figure 9.1—Final Installation of the Boat

Chapter 10
Project 2—Sloop Rig

A sloop is defined as a boat with one mast and one or more sails forward of the mast and a single sail aft of the mast. The sails are generally triangular in shape with the forward sail being referred to as the jib and the aft sail as the mainsail. A sloop with triangular sails is commonly called a Marconi-rigged or Bermuda-rigged vessel. The Bermuda rig was first developed in the West Indies during the 1800's and became extremely popular in the early 1900's for racing yachts because of it's ease of use and the high efficiency gained from the triangular airfoil shape of the sails. The name "Marconi" comes from the fact that the mast, sail and shrouds supporting the mast structure look like a radio tower; hence the term "Marconi" was coined after the inventor of radio and not the inventor of the sailing rig. In any case Sloop, Marconi and Bermuda are correct terms for single masted sailboats with two triangular sails.

The vast majorities of recreational and racing sailboats today are sloop designs and can be found in abundance throughout the world. A Field Guide to Sailboats written by Richard Sherwood describes in words and pictures hundreds of modern sloop designs that are sailing today.

The cover of this book will be used as a guide for the second project. Many of the steps in project 1 will be repeated, but more detail will be added to the hull design including of course the fact that there are two sails instead of one. Since the sloop design is so common, the reader is also encouraged to sketch a hull and sail design of a boat of their choosing or perhaps pattern the model after their own sailboat.

Since much of the process is similar to Project 1, less explanation will be given for each step with concentration only on what is new or different. The same materials from project 1 are used along with the same tools. This project should take about 20 hours to complete, after which the modeler will be experienced enough to tackle more advanced ship designs.

Before starting on the model, it is best to understand how the boat works and how the different parts interact with each other. Figure 10.1 shows the main parts of the sloop. It has a hull with a bow and stern just like the lateen rigged sailboat. The mast is held upright by a forward wire called the head stay and an aft wire called a backstay. The mast is supported on the sides by shrouds. The forward sail is called the jib and the aft sail is called the mainsail. A running line called a sheet controls each sail. A metal spar called the boom supports the lower part of the mainsail. A lifeline helps keep the crew from falling overboard. The bow and stern have a metal railing called a pulpit, which acts to support the lifeline. The keel is usually weighted to keep the boat upright in heavy winds and also to resist sideways motions from the wind. The rudder sets the direction of the boat and is attached to a tiller or ships wheel and is controlled by the helmsman.

Sailboats cannot sail directly into the wind. The sails will luff or flap like a flag when the boat is pointed directly into the wind. As the bow points away from the wind, the sheets are tightened so that the main and jib form an airfoil shape. This is called the close-hauled point of sail and allows the boat to sail into the wind. As the bow falls further away from the wind, the sheets are let out and the boat is on a "reach". When it is directly downwind it is said to be "running". Position the sails of your model to mimic one of the sailing points described above. This will add some realism to your display and give you a better understanding of the function of the running lines and rigging,

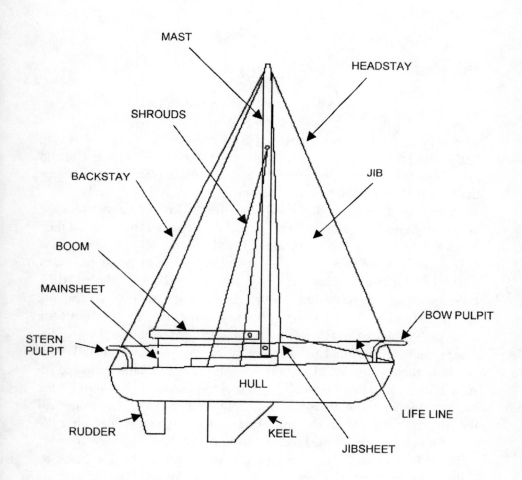

Figure 10.1—Main Parts of the Sloop

Chapter 11
Sloop Hull & Deck

The hull for the sloop is fashioned in the same manner as the lateen rig hull in project 1. Figure 11.1 shows the major dimensions of hull. Cut and sand the hull from a single block of wood. The cabin is made from a 2mm thick strip of wood and glued to the hull as shown in figure 11.1.

After the hull is painted, several holes are drilled into the deck for the various rigging lines. Remember to drill the holes at an angle so that they break through to the bottom of the hull and not through the sides of the hull. Starting at the bow and stern, drill a single hole in the centerline of the hull for the backstay and head stay. Just forward of these holes drill 2 holes on either side of the hull for the stern and bow pulpits. The pulpits are made from 1mm paper clip wire as shown in Figure 11.2. Drill the holes in the hull first and then fit the paper clip into the holes for a snug fit. The pulpit holes are blind and do not go all the way through the hull. Drill one hole each on the left side (port side) of the boat for the main and jib sheets. In the middle of the hull (on top of the cabin), drill two holes for the mast hinge. These holes are blind holes and do not break through all the way to the bottom of the hull. A set of four holes is drilled after the mast for the shrouds. These holes break all the way through to the bottom of the hull at an angle. It is important that this pattern of four holes be drilled after the mast. The mast will be raised and lowered and the shrouds must go slack when the mast is lowered and then tighten when it is in the upright position. See the next chapter, to understand how the shrouds work. Finally, drill 4 holes for the lifeline supports as shown in the figure. The lifeline supports are made from the heads of needles. Cut the needles so they will be at the same height as the pulpit. The lifeline will thread through the eye of the needle.

To complete the hull, glue the hatch covers as shown in Figure 11.2. These covers can be made from thin strips of wood and stained or painted to your liking. Typically hatches are either made of teak wood, or they are made from metal or Plexiglas. If you paint them, gray or black are preferred colors.

The last hole is drilled just forward of the mast. This hole will allow the boom to be pulled up tight to the mast. This will be explained further in the next chapter.

To create the lifeline, start by gluing the bow and stern pulpits in place. The pulpit height is about 3 mm above the deck or 1 mm above the height of the cabin. Make sure the pulpits appear straight and are parallel to the deck. The lifeline is supported by four stanchions, which are essentially fence posts to support the lifeline. The stanchions are made from needles and the eye of the needle is used to support the line. Cut the needles to a length of about 5 mm, such that 2 mm will be sunk into the deck and the height of the needle will be flush with the pulpits. Using gray thread, attach a line from the bow pulpit through the two stanchions and tie it off on the stern rail. Do the same on both starboard and port sides of the boat.

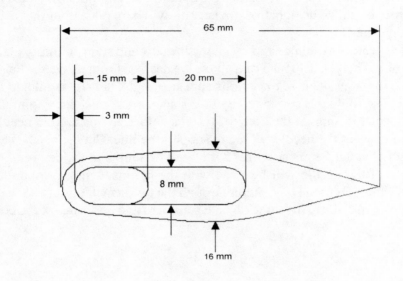

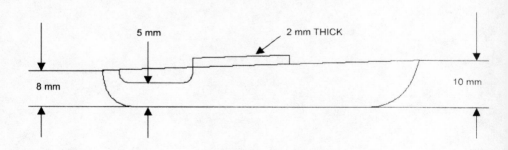

Figure 11.1—Hull Dimensions for Sloop Rig

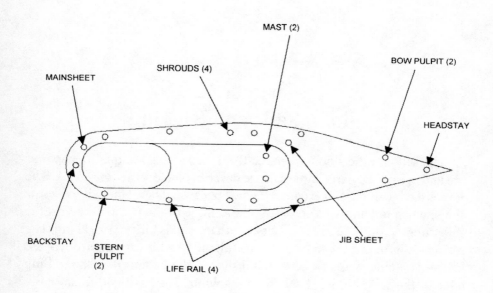

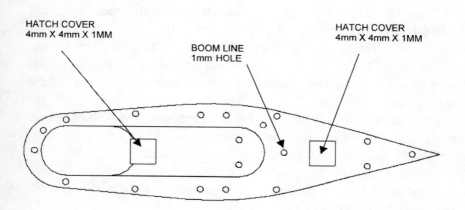

Figure 11.2—Hull Deck Details

Chapter 12
Sloop Sails and Rigging

The sails for the sloop are made from the same good quality paper as the lateen rig. The parts of the sail are described below in Figure 12.1. The forward edge of the sail is called the luff because this is where it looses its shape when not adjusted correctly to the angle of the wind. To adjust the sail properly, the mainsheet is let out until the sail is luffing like a flag. The mainsheet is then drawn in tightly until all the wrinkles are taken out of the sail and it achieve an efficient airfoil shape. The battens help the trailing edge of the sail hold its shape in heavy wind. The head and foot simply refer to the top and bottom. The sail is attached to the mast along the luff of the sail. Use the same method to attach the sail to the mast as you did for the lateen sail to the spar. Do not glue or attach the foot of the main sail to the boom. The sail dimensions are 55 mm along the luff, 25 mm along the foot and 60 mm along the leech. Make sure you glue the mainsheet thread in between the two pieces of mainsail paper and have it dangle from the clew. Refer back to Figure 6.2.

Make the mast and boom from 2 mm diameter dowels, which are 70 mm and 25 mm long respectively. You may stain the dowels to a natural color wood and decorate the sails with rub-on decals used for model railroad trains that are available in most hobby stores as shown in Figure 12.2. The smaller decals look very attractive on the bow to simulate the boats registration number.

Fabricate the jib after making the mast, boom and mainsail. The jib is 75 mm along its luff or forward edge and 15 mm along the foot and 60 mm along the leech or trailing edge of the sail. The jib may be made in two pieces or simply fold the paper in half to form a double thickness. Make sure you draw the seam outlines as shown in Figure 12.2 using a pencil for both the mainsail and the jib. You may add decals to the sails or hull as shown in Figure 12.2.

Before assembling the sails and rigging, study the upper half of Figures 12.2 to become familiar with all of the parts of the assembly. This model is somewhat more difficult than the previous model and there are literally more strings attached. Think about how the boat operates so that when you are rigging each line, you are also thinking about the function too.

Start with the mainsail and mast. The sail should be glued to the mast as previously discussed. Create the mast hinge using 1 mm wire and attach this assembly to the top of the cabin. Take the boom and slide the main sheet (line) through one hole in the end of the boom and tie it off and glue it so that the boom is attached at the clew of the sail and the mainsheet (line) will extend for about 400 mm. Slide the mainsheet thread through the hole in the deck and then attach another line (400 mm) to the other hole in the boom. This line will thread through the hole in the mast that is 6mm from the bottom and then extend through the hole in the hull shown in Figure 12.1. These are the first two lines through the hull, and when pulled will cause the mainsail to take its shape.

Using a single thread, start at the bottom of the hull and create the shrouds by threading through the hull and then through the mast and back again to form two supports or each side of the hull. Hold the mast in the upright position and pull the thread tight and then tie each end together so that the shrouds are a fixed length. When you collapse the mast, the shrouds will go slack and when the mast is vertical the shrouds will be tight and keep the mast from moving too far forward.

Using a one-meter length of thread attach it to the luff of the jib to form the head stay. Also attach a 400 mm length of thread within the jib to form the jib sheet. Thread the lines through the top of the mast to form the backstay and head stay. With the mast in the vertical position, glue and tie the jib head stay to the mast so that when you pull the jib head stay from beneath the hull it will raise the mast until the shrouds are tight. You should have a total of 5 lines going through the hull. These are the backstay, head stay, mainsheet, jib sheet and the forward boom line. This assembly must be able to fit through the neck of the bottle.

Adding N-Scale human figures and a model train brake wheel will add realism to your model. See Figures 12.2 for some ideas. The crew in this picture is daggling their legs over the rail to keep as much weight as possible to the windward side of the boat when sailing close hauled.

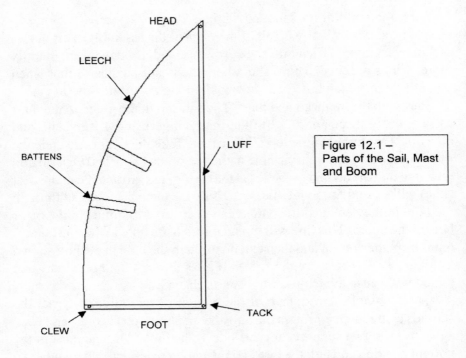

HEAD

LEECH

LUFF

BATTENS

Figure 12.1 –
Parts of the Sail, Mast
and Boom

TACK

CLEW

FOOT

BOOM – 2 mm DIAMETER BY 25 mm LONG – ALL HOLES 1 mm DIAMETER

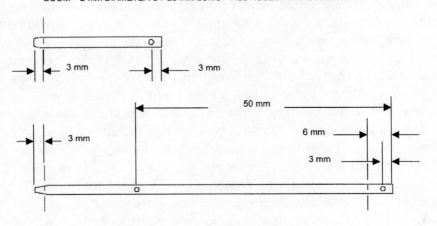

3 mm

3 mm

3 mm

50 mm

6 mm

3 mm

Figure 12.1—Parts of Sail, Mast and Boom

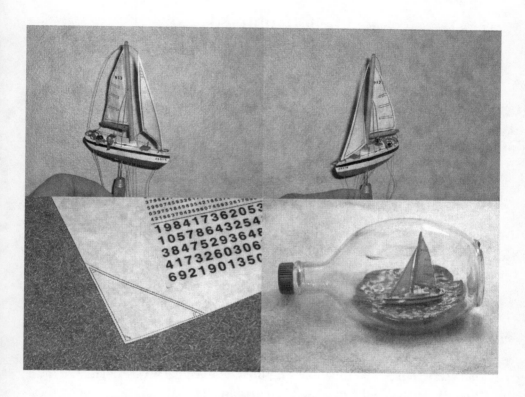

Figure 12.2—Views of Sloop Prior to Installation

Chapter 13
Project 2—Final Installation

When the boat is ready for installation, conduct a trial fit to ensure everything will fit through the neck of the bottle. Fold the mast down and curl the jib slightly to ease the transition through the neck. As mentioned in the previous chapter, the boom is only connected to the main sail at the clew. To fit everything through the neck, the mainsail must be rolled up along with the boom in such a way that all the parts will unravel once inside the bottle.

When ready, heat the bottle from the bottom with a hair dryer so that the clay ocean is soft and pliable. Fold the boat up and slide it through the neck of the bottle. Once inside, use the wire tool to prop up the mast and unravel the sails.

Press the hull gently into the ocean and pull each of the 5 lines gently in the following order. Start with the Headstay as this line will raise the mast to the upright position and tighten the shrouds. Since the lines are being drawn through clay, friction will hold them in place. When the jib and mast are in place, tighten the jib sheet and then gently tighten the backstay, but not so much that it pulls the mast backwards. Tighten the mainsheet so that the main sail is pulled into position. Finally pull on the boom line so that the boom is pulled up snug to the mast.

This entire process takes patience, so move slowly and don't get frustrated. Once everything is in place, put a dab of glue on the jib tack, jib sheet and boom line to ensure that they won't go slack. Let everything dry for 24 to 48 hours and then trim the excess lines with an X-acto knife and touch up the clay with the wire hook tool. This process is identical to what you did on project 1 except with a bit more complexity.

Chapter 14
Additional Projects
Friendship Sloop and Schooner

After reading the previous chapters and building the models, you are now ready to take on more challenging tasks. The two most popular types of ships to model are the Friendship sloop and the Gloucester fishing schooner. Both vessels were extremely popular along the United States east coast during the late 1800's and into the early 1900's. Figure 14.1 shows side plans for each of the vessels. Before taking on these projects it is highly recommended that you examine one of the books in the "Further Reading" section of this book. These more advanced texts on modeling ships in bottles will fill in some of the more intricate details of making these historic vessels.

The Friendship sloop originated from the Muscongus Bay area, off the coast of Maine during the late 1800's. No one knows exactly who invented the classic shape of the hull and rigging, but many credit Wilbur Morse with building many of the boats in the area. Small boatyards were found all around the bay in the towns of Friendship, Friendship Long Island and Bremen Long Island. This boat was very sturdy and would hold up to the severe weather found along the coast of Maine, especially during the winter. The boats ranged from 25 to 40 feet (8 to 12 meters) and were used by small groups of fisherman. The sloop had a single mast with a gaff mainsail and usually two jibs. If you visit Maine today you're likely to see many Friendship sloops still sailing, although for recreational purposes and not for fishing.

The Gloucester fishing schooner was developed in the same part of the United States (Gloucester, Massachusetts) around the mid to late 1800's. These tended to be much larger vessels that were longer than 40 feet (12 meters) and were designed for long harsh voyages off the Grand Banks. The term schooner is used for a ship that has at least two masts, with the forward mast being shorter than the main mast.

You'll notice in the sketches that the jibs are attached to a bowsprit, which extends beyond the bow of a modern sailboat. When placing the model in the bottle, the head stays will be glued to the bowsprit and let to dry before trimming them off. For modeling purposes, the gaff rig sail is not glued to the mast, but is attached to the boom and upper gaff spar. This allows the sail to be rolled up for insertion in the bottle. Other than that, the construction of these boats is similar to what you have learned. The hull, cabin, shrouds, sheets and sails are all made in a similar fashion and function in the same manner as they would on a real vessel.

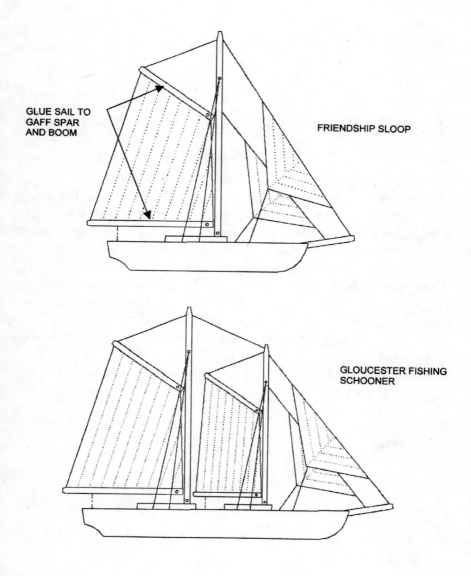

Figure 14.1—Sketches for Gloucester Schooner and Friendship Sloop

Chapter 15
Closing Remarks

There are always new challenges in this hobby. One of the best things about scratch built models is that you don't have to follow the plans, which allows you to come up with unique versions or interpretations of the same basic theme. Project 2 was based on a modern sailing sloop. But sloops come in many sizes and shapes and there are always new ways of making the model fresh and interesting. At the time of this writing, the author has built many ships in bottles, but never one of his own small craft! You can guess what my next project will be.

I hope you'll enjoy this hobby and take the time to model your own boat on the path to learning this wonderful art form. As your skills improve, try some of the more complex models listed in the Further Reading section of this book.

Best Wishes,
Bill Sheridan

Glossary

Backstay—A rigging line that supports the mast to the stern of the boat.

Battens—Wood or Plastic strips that fit into the leech of the sail to hold its shape.

Beam Reach—Sailing at 90 degrees to the direction of the wind

Boom—A wood or metal spar that holds the foot of the sail.

Bow—Front of the boat

Bowsprit—A spar extending from the bow of the boat

Bermuda rig—A boat with one mast and one or more sails forward of the mast and a single sail aft of the mast. Same as Sloop or Marconi rig

Clew—The outer corner of the sail to which the sheet is attached

Close-hauled—Point of sail closest to the direction of the wind.

Foot—Bottom of the sail

Gaff—A spar that supports the head of a sail.

Halyard—A line used to haul sails or spars up and down the mast.

Head—Top of the sail

Headstay—A rigging line that supports the mast to the bow of the boat

Helmsman—The person who steers the boat

Hull—Main body of the boat

Jib—A triangular sail mounted forward of the mast

Keel—A weighted fin mounted to the bottom of the hull, which gives the boat stability from tipping over or moving sideways to the wind.

Leech—The trailing edge of the sail

Lifeline—A wire that surrounds the deck to protect the crew from falling over board.

Luff—The forward edge of the sail.

Luffing—A sail flapping in the wind freely.

Mainsail—A triangular sail mounted aft of the mast on a sloop rig

Mainsheet—A line used for controlling the mainsail.

Marconi rig—A boat with one mast and one or more sails forward of the mast and a single sail aft of the mast. Same as sloop or Bermuda rig.

Port—The left side of the boat

Pulpit—A metal railing at the bow or stern of the boat to protect the crew.

Reach—Sailing with the wind coming over the beam of the boat. Not sailing close-hauled and not running down wind.

Rudder—A flat shaped airfoil normally attached to the stern of the boat, which controls its direction.

Schooner—Vessel with at least two masts with the forward mast shorter than the main mast

Sheet—A line used to control the movement of a sail.

Shrouds—Standing rigging used to support the mast.

Sloop—A boat with one mast and one or more sails forward of the mast and a single sail aft of the mast. Same as Marconi or Bermuda rig.

Starboard—Right side of the boat.

Stern—Rear of the boat.

Stern Rail—Same as Stern Pulpit

Tack—The forward lower corner of the sail where the luff meets the foot.

Tiller—Steering lever attached to the rudder.

Further Reading

• Gary Jobson.1998. *Sailing Fundamentals*. Fireside Publishing
• Bob Bond. 1980. *The Handbook of Sailing*. Alfred A. Knopf Inc.
• Richard M. Sherwood. 1984. *A Field Guide to Sail Boats*. Houghton Mifflin Company
• Ian Dear and Peter Kemp. 1987. *The Pocket Oxford Guide to Sailing Terms*. Oxford University Press.
• Gene Johnson. 1981 Third Edition. *Model Boat Building*. Cornell Maritime Press
• Roger Duncan. 1985. *Friendship Sloops*. International Marine Publishing Company.
• Internet Web Site http://en.wikipedia.org/wiki/Lateen_sail has excellent information on the history of the lateen rig and many other sailboat terms and terminology

Further Reading Books on Ships in Bottles

• Guy DeMarco. 2000 Second Edition. *Ships in Bottles*. Schiffer Publishing Ltd.
• Donald Hubbard. 2004 Second Edition. *Ships-In-Bottles*. Sea Eagle Publishing.
• Jack Needham. 1972. *Modeling Ships in Bottles*. Macmillan Publishing Company.

CPSIA information can be obtained at www.ICGtesting.com
Printed in the USA
LVOW040555120412

277305LV00002B/376/P

9 781424 175970